To Marian—K.R.
To Ben, who gave me my first camera—K.K.

ISBN 0-590-46007-2

Text and photographs copyright © 1991 by Karl Rehm and Kay Koike.
All rights reserved. Published by Scholastic Inc.,
730 Broadway, New York, NY 10003, by arrangement with
Clarion Books, an imprint of Houghton Mifflin Company.

12 11 10 9 8 7 6 5 4 3 2   3 4 5 6 7 8/9

Printed in the U.S.A.   08

First Scholastic printing, October 1993

Left or Right?

Written and Photographed by

Karl Rehm and Kay Koike

SCHOLASTIC INC.
New York Toronto London Auckland Sydney

This is Carrie. This is Sally.

In this picture Carrie is on the left
and Sally is on the right.

Here's Yugo.

Is he on the left or on the right?

Alison has a pink hair tie.

Is Alison on the left or on the right?

Is this merry-go-round horse

on the left or on the right?

Is this little girl in carnival costume

on the left or on the right?

Fresh shrimps for sale!

Are they on the left or on the right?

One spotted cow—

is she on the left or on the right?

Are these big yellow flowers

on the left or on the right?

Is this tiny yellow leaf

on the left or on the right?

Is the big green leaf

on the left or on the right?

Is this tree

on the left or on the right?

Which is your left hand? Which is your right hand?

About This Book

The concept of left and right can bc tricky for young children to master. But once they can identify left and right, they are able to understand and follow certain kinds of directions much more easily—from important safety rules to dance steps to shaking hands.

This book is designed to bring the fun of a puzzle to the process of learning left and right. Locating the objects in the photographs becomes increasingly challenging, but determining whether each is on the left or on the right involves repeating the same choice for every photograph. The final picture invites children to apply the useful concept of left and right to their own hands, and from there to the world around them.

Most subjects were photographed on location in their natural settings in the United States, France, and Germany. All photographs were taken under natural lighting. Karl Rehm used a Nikon FE single-lens reflex camera with Nikon 50mm and 75-150mm zoom lenses with Kodachrome 25 and Fujichrome 50 and 100 ASA films. Kay Koike used a Ricoh XR-M single-lens reflex with 28-105mm Vivitar Series I and 80-200mm Pentax lenses with Ektachrome HC 100 ASA film.

Jacket: The jack-o'-lantern on the jacket back is on the LEFT of the jacket front.
Page 9: Yugo is on the LEFT.
Page 11: Alison is on the LEFT.
Page 13: The merry-go-round horse is on the RIGHT.
Page 15: The girl, dressed for Carnival in Cologne, Germany, is on the LEFT.
Page 17: The shrimps are on the RIGHT. On the left are scallops.
Page 19: This Holstein cow is on the RIGHT.
Page 21: The big yellow chrysanthemums are on the LEFT.
Page 23: The tiny leaf, which is lying on a cobblestone path, is on the RIGHT.
Page 25: The big maple leaf is on the LEFT.
Page 27: The tree is on the RIGHT.